GW00838619

Second Home

Words by Amber Esther,
Beatrice Kitavi & Otis Bolamu

Photography, Commentary &
Design by Joseff Williams

Published in Swansea by Hafan Books in 2021 ©
Hafan Books is a non-profit project for
Swansea Asylum Seekers Support
hafanbooks.org   hafanbooks@post.com

All proceeds from "Second Home" go to
charities that support asylum seekers and
refugees in Wales.

ISBN 978-1-9160442-5-8

Dedicated to those who have
been made to feel unsafe
around the world.

Thanks to Alan Thomas,
Jasmine Green, Jill Duarte,
Kathryn Williams, Ruth Rowley
& Tom Cheesman.

There are approximately 900 people living in Swansea who are classified as "asylum seekers," according to the Home Office. They are men, women and children who have hobbies, family traditions, interests and dreams. Many of them are intellectuals, artists and highly qualified professionals. Before anything else, they are humans and deserve to be treated as such.

Sadly, they are often people who have faced great difficulty and are now looking for a place of safety. They have legitimate and well-founded fears of being persecuted on the grounds of their race, religion, membership of a particular social group or political opinion. Many cannot return to their home countries because protection from oppression, torture, or in some cases, even death cannot be guaranteed.

Confusion occurs for members of the public when those seeking safety are misrepresented by the media under the blanket term of "immigrant." To clarify: an asylum seeker is a person who has applied for asylum and is waiting for a decision on their claim. A refugee has received a positive decision from the authorities on his or her asylum claim.

You may have heard the term "economic migrant." This term does not refer to people seeking asylum.

This term is used to describe someone who moves from one country to another in order to advance their economic and professional prospects. Again, these are not asylum seekers or refugees.

Swansea became the second city in the UK to gain "City of Sanctuary" status in 2010. It is therefore officially recognised as a city that is proud to welcome refugees and asylum seekers, and actively supports their integration into the community.

In this book you will meet three people for whom Swansea has become a second home. They have all experienced living as asylum seekers and, as of 2020, have now received leave to remain. This means they are now allowed to remain in the UK indefinitely or for an allocated amount of time.

You will read of some challenges that perhaps you had no idea people around you have experienced. A good question to ask yourself when reading these stories may be: "What would this be like for me if I was in their situation?"

When you've finished reading, please pass this book onto someone else. We want to ensure that our cities are safe and inclusive places for anyone who is seeking asylum.

AMBER

I had been threatened. I had
been through torture because of
my faith. I didn't want to live
that life for my children.

Amber arrived in the UK from Pakistan in 2012
with her two young children. They were fleeing
a traumatic situation back home. After her
initial interview with the Home Office, Amber
and her children were sent to Cardiff where
they lived for almost a month before being
relocated to Swansea.

Upon moving to Swansea, Amber's local surgery
told her about the African Community Centre,
a local charity providing support to the BAME
community in Swansea. It was here that she
received counselling to process her situation
and gain confidence.

I had thirty
counselling
sessions.

The first few
sessions,
I didn't speak
at all.

"As a counsellor working in this field I am amazed at the courage and resilience that my asylum seeking clients demonstrate. I vowed years ago that I would not complain about my lot after experiencing the horrors that some of my clients face.

From the client who travelled through 22 countries over 12 years and finally received leave to remain in UK, to the young woman who was stowed in a tyre on a ship to escape female genital mutilation. These individuals have so enriched my life and given me a reason to continue working in this field.

I am forever grateful for the wonderful friendships forged and I urge those reading this to join us in helping our fellow humans."

Jill Duarte
Director of the African Community Centre,
and former counsellor to Amber.

Most people categorise us as "immigrant."
They don't understand what asylum is.
They put everyone in the same category.

We don't come here to get people's
jobs. We came here to seek safety.
They don't know that.

People seeking asylum do not come to
work or claim benefits. This is a common
misconception. Most know nothing about
welfare benefits before they arrive and have no
expectation that they would receive any form of
financial support.

Almost all people seeking asylum are not
allowed to work and are forced to rely on state
support. This can mean living on as little as
£5 a day. Living under such tight financial
constraints can go on for months or years
causing great anxiety.

In my experience, Swansea is 99%
racism free. People are accepting of
each other. People know each other.
They say, "Hello!" But whenever I
have found racism, I stood up.
The year before Brexit, a man on
the bus said,

"OH, YOU FOREIGNERS! YOU
SHOULD GO TO YOUR COUNTRY.
SPEAK ENGLISH, DON'T SPEAK
YOUR FOREIGN LANGUAGES

BLAH,   BLAH,   BLAH."

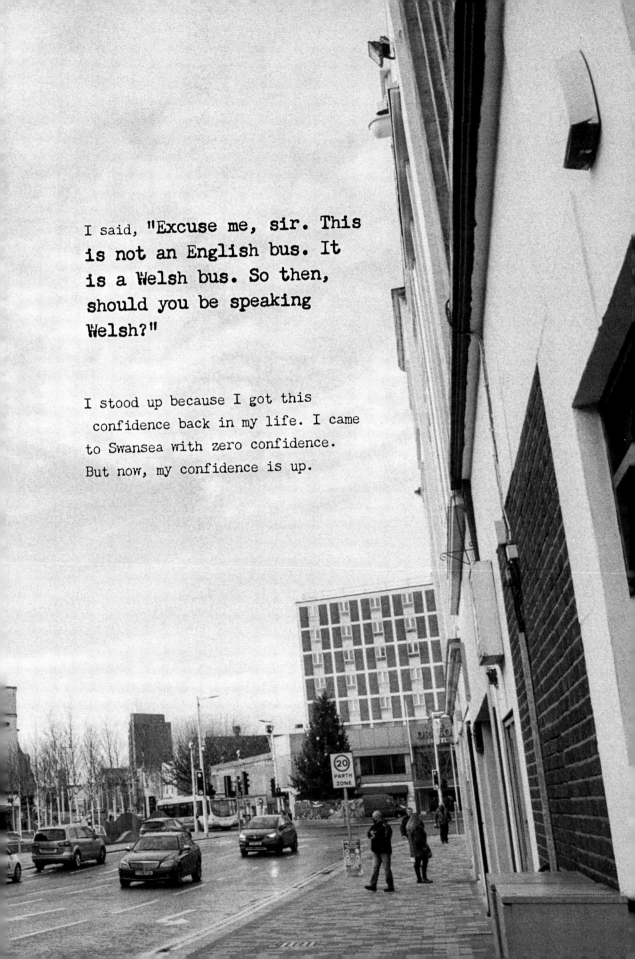

I said, "Excuse me, sir. This is not an English bus. It is a Welsh bus. So then, should you be speaking Welsh?"

I stood up because I got this confidence back in my life. I came to Swansea with zero confidence. But now, my confidence is up.

For most people seeking asylum, their time in the UK is spent in limbo. There is no guaranteed time frame for how long they may be allowed to stay. This makes it somewhat impossible for them to make decisions about their future or make definite plans for their lives.

```
  People judge easily, but they
  don't know what it's like.
```

This has had a direct impact on Amber as a mother of two teenage children. Until very recently, Amber had been waiting for several years to receive the correct paperwork that would allow her daughter to go to university or to get a job. Seeing the affect this has had on her children's lives is a great source of frustration for her.

```
I'm not only a woman, I'm a mother.
People think they are in lockdown.
How about us? My children have been
in lockdown for eight years.
```

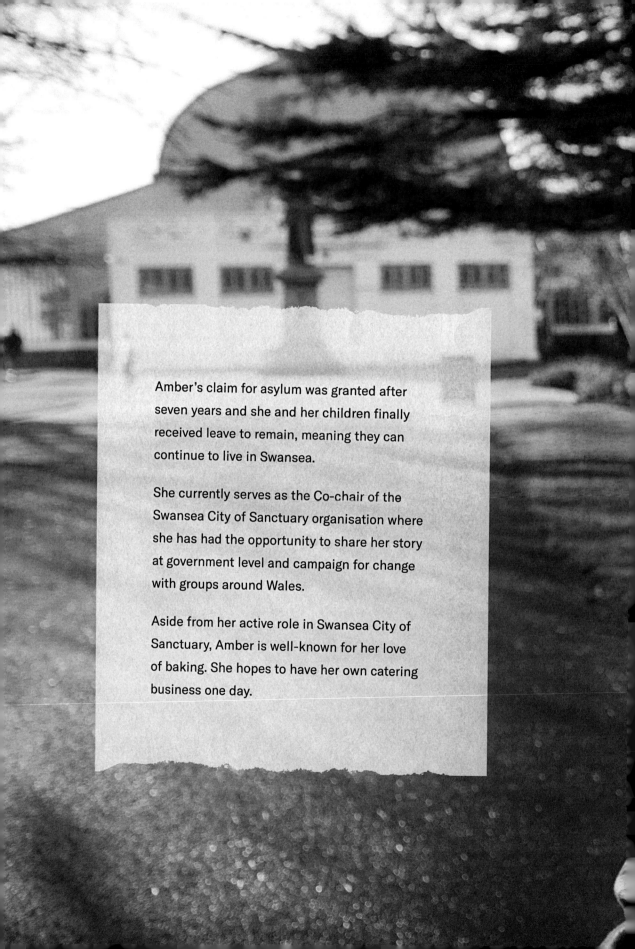

Amber's claim for asylum was granted after seven years and she and her children finally received leave to remain, meaning they can continue to live in Swansea.

She currently serves as the Co-chair of the Swansea City of Sanctuary organisation where she has had the opportunity to share her story at government level and campaign for change with groups around Wales.

Aside from her active role in Swansea City of Sanctuary, Amber is well-known for her love of baking. She hopes to have her own catering business one day.

I was a broken,
    shattered woman.
I am a different woman now.

"I believe Swansea residents should
see asylum seekers and refugees
as new residents in our city who
should be welcomed unconditionally.

We don't welcome and support
refugees because they bring us
benefits or are an asset. We do it
because it is the right thing to do
for fellow human beings in our city
who need some help.

Of course some immigrants of all
sorts do bring benefits - cultural,
economic, new skills, ideas,
insights, enterprising energy,
artistic brilliance and so on. Many
of them are very interesting people
with fascinating stories. They
enrich the social lives of people
who meet them.

But none of that is the motivation
or justification for supporting
people seeking asylum and refugees
in particular."

Tom Cheesman
Trustee, Swansea Asylum Seeker Support

BEATRICE

My heart was anxious at
first. It is not easy
for humans to cope with
drastic change.

Beatrice (or Bie as she is known) is from Kenya.
On arrival to the UK on 22nd December 2018,
Bie discovered that her life was in danger and
that she could not return to her home country.

Bie was allowed to claim asylum in the UK and
was sent to Swansea. People seeking asylum
do not have control over where they can live.
Most aspects of their lives are very much in
the hands of the Home Office. She was given
a room in a shared house in Swansea while
waiting for her claim to be processed.

The first day in Swansea was
uncertain. I didn't know the people
I was living with. I was lonely.

I thought things like, "Are they
going to **accept** me or are they
 going to **reject** me?" It took some
time for me to open up and say,

"My name is Beatrice."

It took me some days to be able to
gain my confidence. Most of the
time I was in my room. Those first
few weeks were lonely days.

Arriving in a new country and sharing a house
with strangers who may have very different
experiences to you can prove challenging for
people seeking asylum, especially when many
are already experiencing trauma themselves.

Initially, Bie had to wait several days to be able
to buy food for herself. One of her housemates
saw that she was struggling and offered some
food she had cooked for herself. This act of
generosity from someone to whom Bie was
effectively a stranger left a lasting impression.

I've experienced
a lot of love.
A lot of love, support and
encouragement in Swansea.
I'm really grateful.

The Welsh people are **very kind** people.
You'll be walking and someone
will just say, "Hello!" and wave.

People go out of their way to help.
They're not even related to you.
They say, "Beatrice, what do
you need?"

Finding a new community can be challenging for many people seeking asylum, particularly where there is a language barrier. However, integration proves extremely beneficial for their mental and emotional well-being in the long term. There are several organisations in Swansea that work to ease the integration process. You can find details of some of these organisations in the closing pages of this book.

For Bie, meeting people of a similar faith was an integral part of her journey. She began attending a local church in Swansea with several other asylum seekers in its congregation. It also offered Bie opportunities to volunteer in supporting the local community. This has helped Bie develop a network of friends she can lean on for encouragement.

Will I find a church where I can
feel **I belong?** It was my top need.
I went there and thought,
 "Oh my God, this is it."

I didn't feel a foreigner.
I felt I belonged.
I felt loved. That gave me
a lot of hope.

Because you're not allowed to work
as an asylum seeker, there's all
these restrictions. It's
as if your mind gets blocked.

     You think, "I have no rights.
     I can't work." Your skills are
     silenced and you're left thinking,
     "What can I do? Nothing. Nothing."

  Now I'm trying to realise, "Oh
  Beatrice, you know, you're skilled
  in this. You're gifted in this."

The long term restrictions placed on people seeking asylum can have challenging affects on their mental health. However, studying at the Bible College of Wales in Sketty has helped Bie to build confidence in her abilities again.

Bie received Humanitarian Protection with five years leave to remain, which means she will be able to live safely in Swansea for five more years before her status is reviewed. Her love of singing and dancing to gospel music has been a great source of encouragement for Bie to remain optimistic through her journey.

It's so important that people interact with us because some of us are very lonely people.

We just want someone to support us and tell us, **"We will walk with you through this new journey."** For me, it was like starting life all over again.

OTIS

When I talk of Swansea,
it's the people. The population.
Swansea, for me, is amazing.
I feel safe.

Otis Bolamu has lived in Swansea since 2017. He is a volunteer at the Oxfam Bookshop on Castle Street. Previously, Otis worked for the electoral commission in his home country, the Democratic Republic of the Congo. During one election season, Otis raised concerns of alleged electoral fraud to the opposition party. He was immediately labelled a suspect of spying for the opposition and was put in severe danger.

For nine days, Otis was imprisoned and tortured. He managed to escape when a family friend bribed a military official. Otis was smuggled out of the Congo and arrived in the UK in October 2017 claiming political asylum immediately. After being initially placed in Cardiff, Otis was moved to Swansea.

In the early hours of the 19th December 2018, Otis was woken unexpectedly and taken from his bed by immigration officers. They took him to a detention centre in Gatwick and told him that he would remain there until Christmas Day, when he would then be deported back to the Democratic Republic of Congo. This was a huge shock to Otis who, until then, had believed that he was safe in Swansea.

When they don't believe you - the government - they kick you out. They tell you that you don't have the right to live here. They will deport you. They will send you back home like,

"WE DON'T WANT YOU. WE DON'T BELIEVE YOU. WE DON'T GIVE YOU THE SECOND HOME."

Maybe back home, if they arrest
you, you come back, they will kill
you. I kept saying to them,

**"No I cannot go back.
I will be killed."**

Otis had built up a network of friends while
volunteering at the Oxfam bookshop. They
quickly rallied to his defence along with
thousands of Swansea residents.

> We were fighting with the
>   government. For me, I didn't
> have the power to fight them.

His case sparked a 60,000 name petition
asking the Home Office to allow him to stay in
the UK. Otis was released from the detention
centre on 10th January 2019. A year later,
Otis was finally granted leave to remain. A
celebration was held in his honour at the Oxfam
bookshop with the wider Swansea community.

> I'm here because of the people of
> Swansea. They fight my case like
> a solicitor and come to my side.

AM's call over battle to halt volunteer's deportation

Liz Perkins
Reporter • 01792 545xxx

AN AM is backing campaigners battling to block the deportation of a popular Swansea-based volunteer.

Bethan Sayed, Plaid Cymru AM for South Wales West, has called on the Welsh Government to support the fight to keep Otis Bolamu in the city, and to work with the Westminster Government to release him from a centre where he was going... fled the Democratic Republic of the Congo after he faced accusations of spying for the opposition in his role as a government worker.

The country has been plagued by periods of political instability, violence and extreme poverty... going... erment to get involved in the case.

She said: "Otis is now an established resident and active member of the community in Swansea.

"He's also volunteered at the Hay Festival, and has a deep care and attachment for his new community. If he returns to the Congo – he could be killed.

"The... UK... reversed. In order to make this happen, everyone needs to keep his story in the news and in everyone's mind, so the UK Government can't deport Otis at some point in the future.

22

Volunteer freed from detention

SOUTH WALES EVENING POST

Refuge

Liz Perkins and Adam Hale

A CONGOLESE charity worker is "overflowing with joy" after winning his battle to remain in Swansea following an outcry by supporters.

Otis Bolamu, 38, is delighted after the Home Office had a change of heart over his asylum application and granted him refugee status.

It was just before Christmas in 2018 that he was originally detained.

The Home Office had planned to deport him to The Democratic Republic of the Congo (DRC) on Christmas Day the same...

Thanks for support in fight against deportation

Bolamu campaign wins right t

Liz Perkins
@lizperkinspost • 01792 545551
elizabeth.perkins@walesonline.co.uk

A CHARITY worker has thanked the people of Swansea for helping him to stay strong in his fight against deportation.

Otis Bolamu, who is still in detention and at risk of deportation, has won support from people backing a petition to keep him in the city.

People are still able to sign in support of him staying in Swansea allowing him to continue to vol-

of other people wh for asylum in Brita put through the brut Britain's immigration

People who ap asylum only have a £37.75 a month to And the money is onto a special 'Azu

West tting was ay in

e 'overflowing with joy'

Otis Bolamu, who has been allowed to stay in Swansea
Picture: Robert Meln

Otis has since used his experience to support
other refugees in Swansea through the
Congolese Development Project.

Here, he works to assist their transition process
and help them integrate into their new lives.
You can find out more about the work Otis does
with the Congolese Development Project by
visiting www.cdpwales.org.uk.

Otis has also been invited by primary schools
to share his story with children to encourage
empathy and inclusion.

Children ask me, "What is an asylum
seeker? What is a refugee?"
I understand they do not know.
I say, "Asylum seekers are the people
who come to ask for a second home."

We often have no idea what the people around us have been through. In order to create cities that are safe for people seeking asylum, it is important that we all question our pre-conceived judgements on people, particularly people who have had a difficult journey.

What are you taking away from reading the experiences of Amber, Bie and Otis?
If you were in an unfamiliar city, with people you did not know, possibly hearing a language you were unfamiliar with, how would you want people to treat you?

To find out more about the ways you can help make Swansea a welcoming place for asylum seekers and refugees, or to learn more about the organisations already doing so, please visit the following websites.

SWANSEA CITY OF SANCTUARY
www.swansea.cityofsanctuary.org

SWANSEA ASYLUM SEEKER SUPPORT
www.sass.wales

AFRICAN COMMUNITY CENTRE
www.africancommunitycentre.org.uk

RACE COUNCIL CYMRU
www.racecouncilcymru.org.uk

WELSH REFUGEE COUNCIL
www.wrc.wales